BIG ENIGMAS

*for Betty Lou Bob —
a fellow writer —
"you are
what you art"
Ken Mikolowski
5/9/97
F.P.L.*

KEN MIKOLOWSKI

PAST TENTS PRESS
DETROIT

Acknowledgments: Some of these poems have appeared in the following publications: BIG SKY, DAILY BARBARIAN, THE FIFTH ESTATE, 48222, HOWLING DOG, THE METRO TIMES, MICHIGAN BROADSIDES, NOTUS, THE PERIODICAL LUNCH, POETRY AGAINST APARTHEID, THE POETRY PROJECT NEWSLETTER, RE; VIEW, ROLLING STOCK, SOUTHPAW, and WAYNE LITERARY REVIEW.

"Tea Time" first appeared as a BILLBOARD POEM co-sponsored by the Poetry Resource Center of Michigan and the Michigan Council for the Arts. Special thanks to project editor Vince Kueter.

Some of these poems were also published in an earlier chapbook, THANK YOU CALL AGAIN, from The Perishable Press.

Thanks to The Michigan Council for the Arts whose Creative Artist Grant assisted the writing of this book.

This book was partially funded by a generous grant from the Mini Grant series of The Michigan Council for the Arts and The Detroit Council of the Arts.

Drawings and back cover photo by Ann Mikolowski.
Cover design by Paul Schwarz

PAST TENTS PRESS
3168 Trowbridge
Hamtramck, Michigan 48212

Printed by CUSHING-MALLOY, INC.
Ann Arbor, Michigan 48107

ISBN 0-9622474-4-8

for Michael and Molly

CONTENTS

POEM   11.
KEN   12.
HOMAGE TO FRANK O'HARA:
Why I am not a New York Poet   13.
HOMAGE TO WILL ROGERS   14.
LAMENT   15.
LAMENT   16.
LAMENT   17.
OVERHEARD AT THE BAR   18.
ALL AT ONCE   19.
TEA TIME   20.
DERRIDA & LADDIDA   21.
DECONSTRUCTION   22.
DID YOU KNOW   23.
LYING IN THE DARK   24.
LIVE IN   25.
MY BIG MOMENT   26.
COMPLETELY UNAWARE   27.
CERTAINLY   28.
ADDICTION   29.
NEUTER GENDER   30.
REMEMBER   31.
NATIONAL ENDOWMENT   32.
OFFCOLOR   33.
ECOLOGY   34.
ECOLOGY   35.
ECOLOGY   36.
LITTLE OR NOTHING   37.
NOT THE BIRD   38.
WAY TO GO   39.
MICHAEL/ALTERNATIVES   40.
WRITING THIS I'VE HALF A MIND   41.
JANUARY IN DETROIT or
SEARCH FOR TOMORROW STARRING
KEN AND ANN   42.
IT'S ALWAYS   45.
IMPERATIVE   46.
UNDERSTANDING POETRY   47.
UNDERSTANDING ART or the power
of the memorable   49.

NOTE TO A BROWSER   52.
HOW IT WORKS   53.
VERBAL SCENARIO   54.
BANNER SPANGLED STAR   55.
BEACH DOVER   56.
EDGAR ALLAN POEM   57.
THIS IS ONE   58.
YOU'RE NOT HERE   59.
MISSING ONE   60.
THINGS TO DO IN AN ECONOMIC CRISIS   61.
THINGS TO DO IN THE OZONE   62.
THINGS TO DO IN GRINDSTONE CITY   63.
THINGS TO DO IN A NUCLEAR DISASTER   64.
GRINDSTONE BLUES   65.
THUMB SCENES   66.
JANUARY IN GRINDSTONE CITY   67.
GRAY LIGHT   68.
DAILY CONSTITUTION   69.
CHAOS   70.
FAMINE   72.
WHY WE ARE IN CENTRAL AMERICA   73.
THE WITNESS   75.
THE LAST POET   76.
NOTHING   77.

BIG
ENIGMAS

POEM

you can't

just write

anything

& call it

a poem

KEN
keeping still, the mountain

I am the youngest son
of the creative &
the representative
of heaven on earth,
dispensing
the blessings
of heaven, the clouds
& rain that gather
round my summit
& thereafter
shine forth
radiant
with heavenly light.

This trigram
shows what modesty is
& how is functions
in a great & strong man.

HOMAGE TO FRANK O'HARA:
Why I am not a New York Poet

Detroit

HOMAGE TO WILL ROGERS

I've

never met

a deadline

I've ever met

yet

LAMENT

I am not now
nor have I ever been

LAMENT

He lived for art
but art did not live for him

LAMENT

I'm just a sheep
in wool's clothing

OVERHEARD AT THE BAR

I'm not
criticizing you
I'm just
pointing out
the discrepancies
in your life

ALL AT ONCE

It's time to take the cure
I think I'd rather take a tour

TEA TIME

a cup sits on the table
nearby is a tea pot
from it a tiny submarine emerges

DERRIDA & LADDIDA

Poetics makes
bedfellows estranged

DECONSTRUCTION

all the king's horses
and all the king's men
couldn't put a poem
back together again

DID YOU KNOW

Martin Gautman's wife
dyed her hair red
and when it got there
she left him

LYING IN THE DARK

left ear on the pillow

right ear cocked/

                listening

the dog/ barking

something moving around

                   downstairs

welcome mr burglar

LIVE IN

I want to live in
Blissful Ignirance,
Alabama

MY BIG MOMENT

Camera points this way
Red light blinks on
"Hello #1. We're Mom!"

COMPLETELY UNAWARE

In May of 1975
rushing into a subway station
completely unaware
Mary Clare Uhanak ran into
a perfect stranger.

Fifteen years later
on a late fall day
In front of the Metropolitan Museum of Art
in the same city
that same stranger
still perfect
ordered two hot dogs
with mustard and sauerkraut
before rushing into the Futurist exhibit.

CERTAINLY

We have
always lived
our lives
with a certain
abandon
she said
as she packed
her bags
I am certain
you will
understand

ADDICTION

Fighting a losing battle
lives next door
to a vibrant woman
in her 30's.
When he talks to her
sub-mediocre takes over
in a big way.
Zombie-ized by the big eye
she even sleeps with it on.
Just sign me: concerned.

NEUTER GENDER

Your lip
on it
is it
itself

REMEMBER

smut

is just

tums

spelled backwards

NATIONAL ENDOWMENT

The Wedding Dance

by Brueghel

is almost

identical

to the postcard

reproduction

except for a few

noticeable lower extremities

which protrude

from the male

characters

not shown

on the postcard

OFFCOLOR

When a white officer

was attacked

by a black inmate

fellow troopers

blasted the assailant

at such close range

that the officer

himself

was pinked.

ECOLOGY

some

day

soon

nothing

will be

made

out of

wood

not

even

trees

ECOLOGY

the earth is round
like a ball
industry raises its racket
prepares to serve

ECOLOGY

you &

me &

every

thing

LITTLE OR NOTHING

there are these trees.
and beyond these trees,
trees. and beyond that
little or nothing. little
fields and nothing but sky.

NOT THE BIRD

but the shadow of the bird
flying

WAY TO GO

Gone

MICHAEL/ALTERNATIVES

you dont owe for your skin
your toes
teeth, your blood are free
take the food you need
grow
youll be loved
work at what you please
laugh
greet the sun each day
you dont owe for your soul

WRITING THIS I'VE HALF A MIND

Writing this I've half a mind
to stop and look for you. Listen,
that sounds the better idea by far.

But you are about to start on some
new piece of art. So I won't go
just now to seek you out. But

often as not I've done just that. That's
what I mean I've half a mind
to find you anyway. You wouldn't mind

so much. Say half way through a book
I'd look up and find you there why
I'd put that book aside just like that.

And that's why I shouldn't even try
right now. Right or wrong, you'd go
along with whatever thought I had in mind.

Tight as we are I might as well admit
to it and let you be for now. Get
you right out of mind for half an hour or so.

JANUARY IN DETROIT or
SEARCH FOR TOMORROW STARRING KEN AND ANN

I think it is interesting
though not exactly amusing
how we go from day to day
with no money. How do we
do it, friends ask, suspecting
we really have some stash
stacked away somewhere.
But we certainly do not
and we also do not know
how we do it either.
You sure are lucky,
some of our friends say. I am
none too sure of that though,
as I wait for the winning
lottery numbers to be announced
on CKLW. Thursday in Detroit
is the day of dreams. We have
been dreaming of a place
in the country lately and I'm
none to sure that is very healthy.
And speaking of health that's
also been a problem that probably
has something to do with no money,
since we've all been sick lately,
taking turns politely of course.
Could you bring me some more
tea one of us will ask,
and the other will.
In between the coughing and
worrying our thoughts
have often turned to crime.
We seriously wonder how we can
get away with a bundle with
as little risk as possible.
Last week we took our last
$12 out of the bank
and noticed how much more
they had there though
we had none. Of course

we wouldn't rob that bank,
they know us there
as the ones who bring
the rolls of pennies in.
And just yesterday they
fish-eyed us for trying
to cash our son's xmas bond
from his grandparents
after only one month.
So we wouldn't try to rob that bank,
but I do know of one up north
that may be possible...
I know this just seems like
romantic dreaming
but I practically make a career
of reading detective stories,
and God knows, I have no other.
Anyway if the right opportunity
comes along, we are more
than ready to meet it.
But this is a time of waiting,
the I Ching says, though it does
not say how we are to eat
while waiting. And soon
we will have another mouth to feed—
Ann now in her seventh month,
and that is often in our thoughts.
Besides all that we are both
over thirty, artist and poet,
still waiting to cross the great water.
Meanwhile, day after day,
there is still Detroit
to be dealt with—a small pond
says our friend Snee.
Big fish we used to answer him,
but that was a while back.
Now we think maybe Lake Erie
is the great water referred to
in the I Ching, and if we wait
long enough we can
walk across—to Buffalo
or Cleveland. In a healthy person,
says the philosopher, self-pity

can be a forerunner to action:
once the problem is seen clearly,
a solution may be found at hand.
And as I said, I think it is interesting
though not exactly amusing.

IT'S ALWAYS

darkest
before you
turn
the lights on

IMPERATIVE

to move
> foreward

> or otherwise
> but
to move
> anyway

somehow
> soon or
even now
surely
> we must
or not

UNDERSTANDING POETRY
for Brenda Goodman

made with skill
packed with care
easy to assemble
ready to use
saves you time
and effort

this poem comes
in decorator colors
to be hung above the couch
admired by visitors

roaches are red
violins are blue
this poem is so meaningful
cause it's just for you

poems not exceeding 72 inches
length and girth combined
and not over 40 pounds in weight
are mailable to all points
within the United States

what has poetry done for you
lately

this poem seems to give
a great deal of good advice
it tells the reader not to waste
his time but to be up and doing
not to be discouraged by failures
but to have a heart for any fate
not to judge life by temporary standards
but to look to eternal reward
there are probably few people
who would quarrel with the moral value
of these statements
however

we can still ask whether or not
the poem is a good poem

do you seek a pleasant poem
look about you

get it
or do I have to draw a picture for you

UNDERSTANDING ART
or the power of the memorable
for John Egner

it appears
among us
as red
does

*

it adheres

*

the reading
of the possible
meaning
of that

*

a specific
demand
in art

*

that aint
no statue
of liberty

*

yet fundamentally
the form
persists

*

strangely unaccountable

*

permitted to feel
they felt

*

they were more
organically
present than we

*

1-2-3-4-5

*

the painting of
a feeling
that is a
person

*

how do you do

*

that form
does not
look
like grandmother

*

put some
chrome
on it

*

we want
to live
too

*

we shift
the credits
and debits
around
so no one
knows

*

the meaning
is somewhere
so we hit
everywhere

*

naples yellow
vermillion
blue, red
orange

*

wouldn't it be
wonderful
if the whole
thing were
like the good part

*

the humor
in the word
genius
is not always clear

*

you are
what you art

*

but please
don't call it
mysticism

*

the whole
block runs out
to tell
everyone
there's been
an earthquake

NOTE TO A BROWSER

leafing
through these pages
looking
for something short

here it is

HOW IT WORKS

look
lift
turn
pull
drop
drag
ask
wait
&
wonder

VERBAL SCENARIO

works
was
came
said
fill

got
checked
washed

received

was

would
lean
was
driving
went

had driven
waited
help

breathed
said
suppose
want

had said
filled

would
look
asked

gave
looked
longed

drove

BANNER SPANGLED STAR

Hailed we proudly so what
Light early dawns the by
See you can say Oh

BEACH DOVER

By night clash armies ignorant where
Flight and struggle of alarms confused with swept
Plain darkling a on as here are we and
Pain for help nor peace nor certitude nor
Light nor love nor joy neither really hath
New so beautiful so various so
Dreams of land a like us before lie to
Seems which world the for another one to
True be us let, love, Ah!

EDGAR ALLAN POEM

This is no nightmare. Mother
will not wake you with oatmeal
and say dreams are all in your head.
The boogieman is real.
He is going to eat us all.

THIS IS ONE

this is too

YOU'RE NOT HERE

you're not there

MISSING ONE

too much
makes one
miss too much

THINGS TO DO IN AN ECONOMIC CRISIS

Buy low

Stay high

THINGS TO DO IN THE OZONE

Rub gently

THINGS TO DO IN GRINDSTONE CITY

Look at the sky
my oh my

THINGS TO DO IN A NUCLEAR DISASTER

Say hello to Ted

GRINDSTONE BLUES

There
isn't
much
to
do
in
Grindstone
City
but
then
you
never
get
the
chance
anyway

THUMB SCENES
for John Sinclair

ubly girl
reigns as
kinde bean queen

pigeon elevator
boosts
local economy

hemans
hosts bad axe
right to lifers

pinnebog couple
suffers
car deer mishap

oh john
if you lived here
you'd be home now

JANUARY IN GRINDSTONE CITY

I think it is amusing
now that we're healthy
we're dreaming of a place
in the city.

GRAY LIGHT

speaks
cold metal

smoke
spoke
trails

a hum
more
a buzz

DAILY CONSTITUTION

let us not disturb

the sound sleep

of the people

by the people

and for the people

CHAOS
for Bob Sestok

Horror
upon horror
& all in a hurry
a rush of words
a flash of time passing
a rhythm of flow & flow & flow
& then a pause
of serenity & recollection
& then further flow of fast time passing
& events passing
& history now here & now gone
with no let up
only here & there a pause
a moment
then just everything in general
flowing past
events & people
moving through chaos
nothing
to put your finger on nothing
to stop the chaos
nothing to break the flow of chaos
or horror of events
or people or time
except here or there something special
something personal in the flow
a moment only
& then the flow again
the flow toward the ultimate
the bigger horror
the more violent violence
the final perfect moment to total horror
& total chaos
what we've all been waiting for
what we know is there
waiting for us
each of us
in a personal moment of total clarity

caught in the general flow of horror.
There.
That one—that's me.

FAMINE

apples
and oranges
and
bananas
are so many
nuts and
bolts

WHY WE ARE IN CENTRAL AMERICA

because there are
issues to debate
orders to delegate
borders to defend
dominoes to deflect
jungles to defoliate
missiles to deploy
nuns to deflower
rumors to denounce
atrocities to deny
situations to defuse
theories to debunk
minerals to desire
resources to deplete
profits to deposit
currencies to devalue
overruns to defray
coffee to decaffinate
diplomats to debrief
rights to deny
elections to delay
churches to desecrate
despots to deify
peoples to debase
bureaucracies to departmentalize
parameters to delineate
documents to declassify
computers to deprogram
workers to debilitate
rebels to demobilize
sympathizers to demoralize
zones to demilitarize
buildings to demolish
villages to destroy
areas to depopulate
corpses to decompose
bombs to detonate
wars to declare
children to deprive
to deform

dehumanize
desist
desist
desist

THE WITNESS

someday they'll bring you in
as a witness
after all you watched it happen
you were there
maybe you were even an accomplice

did you go to college
to be competitive in today's market
learn from professors who research star wars

did you or did you not see
riot police in south africa beat heads
watch ethiopians starve on the evening news

were you or were you not a good consumer
wear the latest fashions and say charge it
eat a nice lunch at a new cafe

did you take a trip to mexico
when the peso was devalued
benefit from reaganomics

think we should
protect our interests in latin america
take in a good film tonight

were you a witness or just another victim
it won't make any difference
you were there
weren't you

THE LAST POET

I want to write

the last poem

be writing

the last poem

when it happens

be known as

the writer of

the last poem

NOTHING

can replace

poetry

in my life

and one day

surely

it will

Ken Mikolowski is the author of two previous collections of poetry: **THANK YOU CALL AGAIN** (The Perishable Press) and **little mysteries** (Toothpaste Press). He teaches poetry writing at the Residential College of the University of Michigan in Ann Arbor. Along with his wife and partner, Ann, he is the editor, publisher and printer of The Alternative Press.